T0413243

SPACE EXPLORATION

BEYOND THE SOLAR SYSTEM

by Christine Marie Layton

BrightP★int Press

San Diego, CA

© 2023 BrightPoint Press
an imprint of ReferencePoint Press, Inc.
Printed in the United States

For more information, contact: BrightPoint Press
PO Box 27779
San Diego, CA 92198
www.BrightPointPress.com

LIBRARY OF CONGRESS CATALOGING-IN-PUBLICATION DATA

Names: Layton, Christine Marie, author.
Title: Beyond the solar system / by Christine Marie Layton.
Description: San Diego, CA : BrightPoint Press, [2023] | Series: Space exploration | Includes
    bibliographical references and index. | Audience: Grades 10-12
Identifiers: ISBN 9781678204242 (hardcover) | ISBN 9781678204259 (eBook)
The complete Library of Congress record is available at www.loc.gov.

CONTENTS

AT A GLANCE

- The solar system contains the Sun and all the objects that orbit around it, such as planets, moons, and asteroids.

- The heliosphere is the area around the Sun that is influenced by the Sun's magnetic field and particles coming from the Sun. Beyond the heliosphere is interstellar space.

- Scientists believe the Oort Cloud lies beyond the heliosphere. It is made up of small, icy bodies that orbit the Sun at a great distance.

- A telescope is a tool that makes faraway objects seem much closer. Telescopes in space can provide clear images of distant galaxies. Telescopes on Earth do not provide as clear of a view. This is because Earth's atmosphere is in the way.

- The James Webb Space Telescope launched in 2021. It is the most advanced space telescope yet.

- A probe is a robotic spacecraft that travels through space collecting data. The probe sends the data back to Earth. Only a few probes have reached interstellar space.

- Sending probes to interstellar space takes a very long time. Scientists are designing interstellar probes that can travel more quickly and efficiently.

- There are no current plans to send humans beyond the solar system. Scientists must overcome major challenges to make such a voyage possible.

INTRODUCTION

INTERSTELLAR SPACE EXPLORATION

A probe sails through **interstellar space**. It is billions of miles from the Sun. The probe gathers information as it travels. It sends this **data** back to Earth for scientists to study.

The probe's original mission was to study the outer planets. It flew past Jupiter and

Saturn. But the probe was not designed to stop there. It kept going. Decades later, it reached interstellar space.

This is a cold, dark place. There is nothing to photograph. But the probe can still collect scientific data. It detects magnetic fields and measures particles.

It takes many years for a probe to reach interstellar space.

It will keep sending this data back to Earth as long as it can.

Eventually the probe will run out of power. It will go silent. After completing its amazing mission, it will continue drifting through interstellar space for millions of years.

WHAT IS INTERSTELLAR SPACE?

The solar system contains the Sun and everything that **orbits** it, such as planets, moons, and asteroids. The Sun releases particles called the solar wind. The solar wind acts like a big bubble around the solar system. This bubble forms the heliosphere.

BOUNDARIES OF THE SOLAR SYSTEM

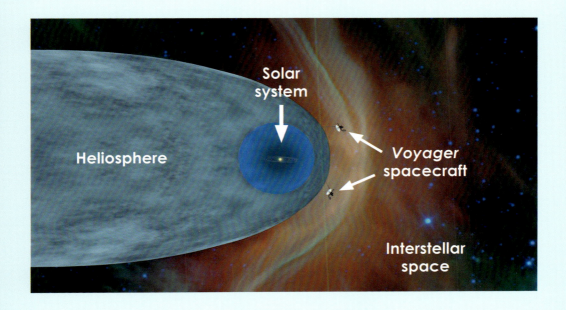

Solar system

Heliosphere

Voyager spacecraft

Interstellar space

The heliosphere surrounds the solar system. The Voyager spacecraft have flown beyond the heliosphere and into interstellar space.

Distance in space is measured in astronomical units (AU). One AU is equal to the average distance between Earth and the Sun. This is about 93 million miles

(150 million km). The nearest edge of the heliosphere is about 120 AU from the Sun.

Beyond the heliosphere is interstellar space. Gases and dust move through interstellar space. Scientists study these materials to find out how the universe formed.

The Oort Cloud is made up of icy bodies that orbit the Sun. Scientists believe it is located outside the heliosphere. It may extend as far as 100,000 AU from Earth. Comets may form there.

A few probes have reached interstellar space. In the future, scientists will design

Comets can sometimes be seen from Earth. Dust and gases stream from the comet, forming a colorful tail.

more missions to explore interstellar space. Scientists are interested in this region for many reasons. It can give clues about how the solar system formed. It can help scientists learn more about how the universe works.

1

EXPLORING WITH TELESCOPES

Scientists can use telescopes to explore beyond the solar system without leaving Earth. A telescope is a tool that makes distant objects appear closer. By looking at light from distant objects, a telescope looks back in time. Light travels at a constant speed. The light from a faraway star may take millions of years to reach Earth. The

scientist is seeing the star as it looked

millions of years ago.

Early telescopes used glass lenses.

The lenses helped **magnify** the image.

The first telescope was made in Europe in

1608. Inventors placed two lenses about

Telescopes today can be very large.

12 inches (30 cm) apart from each other.

The first lens gathered light from far away.

It focused the light to a point. The second

lens spread the light out across the eyeball.

This made the distant object appear larger.

In 1609, Italian scholar Galileo Galilei

used a telescope to look at the night sky.

He built his own telescope. His first version

magnified objects three times. He improved

his lenses until they magnified the view thirty

times. He made many discoveries using his

telescope design. He learned that the Moon

is not a perfect sphere. He also discovered

some of Jupiter's moons.

Galileo Galilei was an astronomer, mathematician, and inventor.

Telescopes continued to improve. Inventors used bigger lenses that could magnify more. But bigger glass lenses also caused problems. The thick lenses made the telescope heavy. They also affected the color of the view. This is because of how light bends through the lenses. Telescopes needed to be very long. Large lenses need to be placed far apart to focus light. The length made the telescopes even heavier.

English scientist Isaac Newton solved these problems in 1668. He invented a reflector telescope. This kind of telescope uses mirrors instead of glass lenses. Mirrors do not affect color. They helped telescopes become more lightweight. They could focus light without the telescope being very long.

An observatory is a building that has a large telescope. Observatories have tools

Most telescopes today are reflector telescopes. They are based on Isaac Newton's design.

that help scientists study space from Earth. In 1924, American scientist Edwin Hubble worked at Mount Wilson Observatory in California. He used the Hooker Telescope to look far beyond the solar system. It was the most powerful telescope in the world at the time. He discovered other galaxies.

SPACE TELESCOPES

Telescopes work by gathering light. Earth's **atmosphere** blocks some light. It can make the view of space hazy. Space telescopes orbit above Earth's atmosphere.

HENRIETTA SWAN LEAVITT

Certain kinds of stars change in brightness over time. This change can be used to calculate how far away these stars are from Earth. Henrietta Swan Leavitt was the scientist who made this discovery. Her method helped astronomers measure the size of the Milky Way. Edwin Hubble used her method to measure the distance to other galaxies.

They can get a clearer view of objects in space.

The National Aeronautics and Space Administration (NASA) began to launch space telescopes in 1966. Early versions were called Orbital Astronomical Observatories (OAOs). They needed power to **transmit** information back to Earth. But the first one never turned on. The power did not work.

OAO 2 launched in 1968. It was a success. It became the first telescope to work in space. Scientists controlled the telescope from Earth. But it was hard

In 1968, scientists tested equipment that would be used for OAO 2.

to operate. It was circling the planet at

thousands of miles per hour. "OAO 2 was

a learning experience," said Nancy Grace

Roman. She was the first chief of astronomy

at NASA. "We had to learn how to point a telescope to a single object and hold it there for a half-hour or so." [1]

In 1990, the Hubble Space Telescope (HST) launched into orbit. It was the largest space telescope yet. It was about the size of a school bus. Scientists named it after Edwin Hubble. The HST improved on earlier tools in many ways. Its main mirror is 7.9 feet (2.4 m) wide. It lets the telescope see amazingly distant objects. It can see far beyond the solar system. The HST has observed many stars and galaxies. It helps scientists learn more about the universe.

NASA scientists planned for astronauts to make regular repairs to the HST. But the first repair came right away. Its mirror had a flaw. Images were coming back fuzzy. Astronauts repaired the telescope in 1993. Soon the images were coming back sharp and clear. Later missions upgraded the HST to make it even better. In 2020,

OTHER GALAXIES

The Milky Way Galaxy is home to Earth's solar system. It also contains billions of other stars that have their own solar systems. Scientists once thought the Milky Way was the only galaxy in the universe. Today's scientists estimate that there are more than 100 billion galaxies in the universe.

NASA celebrated the telescope's thirtieth anniversary. It was still going strong.

MODERN SPACE TELESCOPES

The James Webb Space Telescope (JWST) launched in 2021. It is ten times more powerful than the HST. It will help scientists study distant galaxies and stars. It will also look for planets in other solar systems.

The HST is only 350 miles (563 km) above Earth. The JWST is nearly 1 million miles (1.6 million km) away. It is too far away for astronauts to visit it and make repairs.

A powerful rocket carried the James Webb Space Telescope to space.

The telescope is designed to keep working on its own for many years.

One improvement is the mirror. The JWST mirror is larger than the HST mirror. It is divided into eighteen parts. They unfolded after launch to form one large mirror. This design made the mirror easy to launch. It took up less room than a single mirror of the same size.

The JWST has a sun shield the size of a tennis court. It keeps the telescope cool. This is needed to keep its sensitive equipment working properly.

Engineer Sandra Irish worked on the JWST. She compared the telescope to the HST in an interview. Irish said, "JWST goes beyond Hubble Space Telescope in searching back in time to understand the first light of the universe and galaxies being formed."[2]

2

EXPLORING WITH PROBES

A probe is a robotic spacecraft. No people are on board. It travels through space and collects data. This data may be in the form of photos. It may be information about the particles or magnetic fields the probe encounters. The probe sends all this data back to Earth.

The Soviet Union launched *Sputnik 1* in 1957. This probe orbited Earth. It was the first human-made object in space. The United States launched a probe called *Explorer 1* the next year. It also orbited Earth.

The Explorer 1 probe orbited Earth more than 58,000 times.

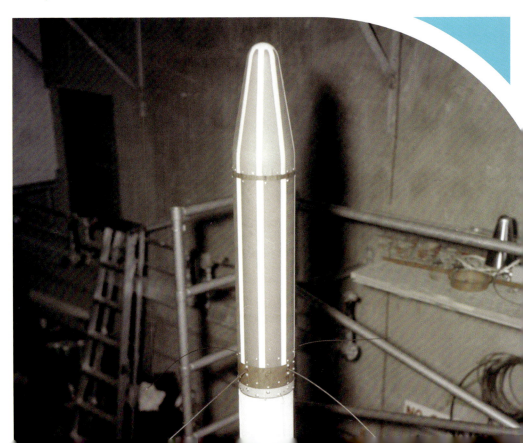

Early probes collected data about Earth from space. Scientists learned a lot from these missions. They learned how to reach Earth orbit. They learned how to send data back to Earth. Technology improved. Scientists began to design probes for longer missions beyond Earth orbit.

PROBE PROGRESS

In the 1960s, probes began exploring the solar system. *Mariner 2* flew past Venus in 1962. It was the first probe to study another planet. *Mariner 4* flew past Mars in 1965. It sent back pictures of the planet's craters.

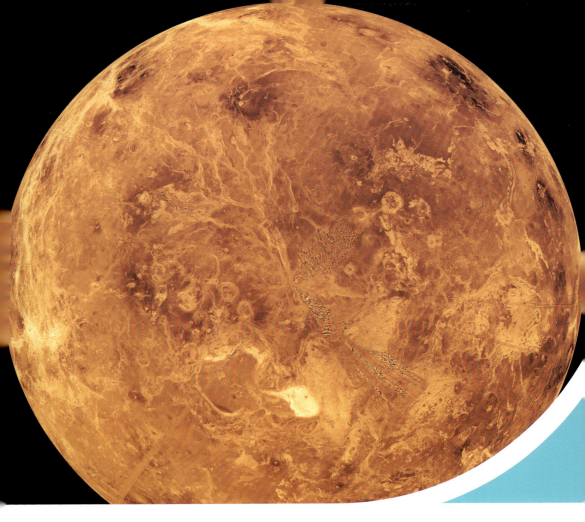

The first NASA flyby probe helped scientists learn more about Venus.

Mariner 9 was the first probe to orbit a

planet other than Earth. It entered Mars

orbit in 1971.

This illustration depicts Pioneer 10 *flying past Jupiter.*

As time went on, scientists developed more advanced probes. These new missions explored the outer solar system. *Pioneer 10* launched in 1972. It became the first probe to study Jupiter up close.

Pioneer 11 followed in 1973. It flew past both Jupiter and Saturn.

After studying these planets, the *Pioneer* probes continued onward. They kept sending back data on their way out of the solar system. *Pioneer 11* sent its last signal in 1995. *Pioneer 10* last contacted Earth in 2003. The dead spacecraft are still travelling into interstellar space.

LEAVING THE SOLAR SYSTEM

Voyager 1 and *Voyager 2* are probes that launched in 1977. *Voyager 1* flew past Jupiter and Saturn. *Voyager 2* studied

Jupiter, Saturn, Uranus, and Neptune. This exploration program was successful. As with the *Pioneer* probes, the *Voyager* spacecraft continued their journeys.

The *Voyager* probes continue to send data back to Earth. The spacecraft can measure particles coming from the Sun. A change in these measurements tells scientists when a probe has left the heliosphere. *Voyager 1* exited the heliosphere in August 2012. *Voyager 2* followed in November 2018.

Scientists expected that the probes would have enough power to keep sending

Voyager 2 helped scientists learn more about Neptune, Uranus, Saturn, and Jupiter (left to right).

data until the mid 2020s. These probes

are the first active human-made objects to

reach interstellar space. They have given

scientists valuable information about what

this region is like. Scientist Jim Bell has

written about the *Voyager* probes. He said, "It's just very exciting to be able to literally enter interstellar space. And along with the spacecraft we've all entered the interstellar age . . . because now we have interstellar travelers among us."[3]

THE GOLDEN RECORD

Voyager 1 and *Voyager 2* each contain a recording called the Golden Record. It is filled with information about Earth. The record has photographs, greetings in many languages, and the sounds and music of Earth. If intelligent lifeforms ever find the probes, they could learn what Earth is like.

The *New Horizons* probe is following earlier spacecraft out of the solar system. It launched in 2006. Its mission was to study the dwarf planet Pluto. *New Horizons* reached Pluto in 2015. It collected valuable images and data as it flew past. Then it continued toward interstellar space. In April 2021, it reached an important milestone. It became the fifth spacecraft to reach a distance of 50 AU from the sun. Scientists predict it will leave the heliosphere in the mid-2040s.

3

WHAT'S NEXT IN INTERSTELLAR EXPLORATION?

The *Voyager* probes reached interstellar space. But this was not their main goal. They lose electrical power over time. Eventually they will stop working. Future scientists will build probes specifically for interstellar travel.

CHALLENGES FOR INTERSTELLAR PROBES

There are many challenges to building

interstellar probes. Distance is the biggest

one. The edge of the heliosphere is

extremely far away. Probes built with today's

Voyager 1 *was the first active probe to reach interstellar space.*

Workers assemble a J-2X engine. This powerful engine will be used on space missions beyond Earth orbit.

technology take several decades to get there. Long missions have a greater risk of something going wrong.

Even with new engines and power sources, interstellar missions will likely take a long time. Ralph McNutt works in the Applied Physics Laboratory at Johns Hopkins University. His team is working on plans for an interstellar probe. McNutt knows the probe may not give results in his lifetime. He said:

> *Suppose this thing launched in 2036, and it got to the end of the . . . mission in 2086. That puts me at about 130 years old. I'm not going to worry about it. You have to hand these things off. I say to people, "If you're into instant gratification, do not get involved with space exploration."* [4]

Leaving the solar system is one thing. But reaching the nearest star would be even harder. The edge of the heliosphere is about 120 AU away. The nearest star is Proxima Centauri. It is about 270,000 AU away. A spacecraft going at *Voyager 1*'s speed would take over 73,000 years to get there.

Power is another problem. Probes need electricity to send data back to Earth. The *Voyager* probes and *New Horizons* use a radioisotope thermoelectric generator (RTG). An RTG contains radioactive material. It gives off heat over time. The RTG turns this heat into electricity. This method

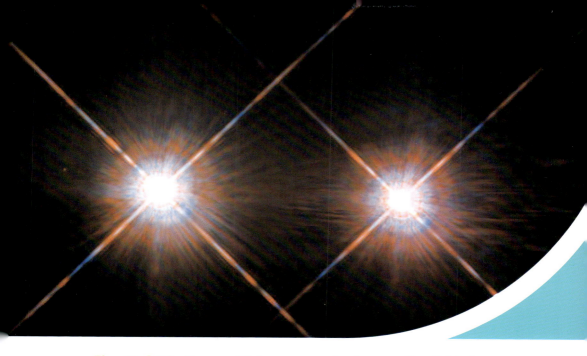

The Hubble Space Telescope photographed Alpha Centauri A (left) and Alpha Centauri B (right), two of the stars closest to our solar system.

can produce power for decades. But an interstellar mission may take even longer than that.

SOLVING THE PROBLEMS

Scientists are thinking of solutions to the problems of distance and power. Several teams are working on designs for interstellar probes. Their designs would improve on earlier spacecraft. Unlike the *Voyager* probes, they would be made specifically for interstellar missions.

McNutt's team is designing an interstellar probe that would travel faster than the *Voyager* probes. A powerful rocket would launch the probe. The probe will fly by

POWER IN SPACE

For missions close to the Sun, spacecraft often use solar panels to generate power. But beyond Jupiter, sunlight is too faint for solar panels. Long-range space missions often use RTGs instead. They are also useful for rovers on Mars, where dust may block sunlight.

Jupiter. It will use the planet's gravity to pick up more speed. It would reach a top speed of 6 to 7 AU per year.

McNutt's design also includes an improved power system. NASA is developing better RTGs using new materials. These could provide power for 100 years. This would let the probe stay in contact with Earth for much longer.

BREAKTHROUGH STARSHOT

Another team is developing a more advanced interstellar probe. The name of this program is Breakthrough Starshot.

Astronomer Avi Loeb of Harvard University is working on the probe. It is designed to reach the nearest star. The idea is in the early planning stages. But scientists are beginning to figure out how it might work.

Breakthrough Starshot would involve a tiny probe with the mass of a paper clip. It would have a sail on it. A laser on Earth would shine on the sail. This would push the probe forward. Over time, the little probe could reach amazing speeds. It could reach Proxima Centauri in just 20 years. Loeb's team imagines sending thousands of these probes at once.

Breakthrough Starshot will have a design similar to a solar sail (pictured). Solar sails use light from the Sun to pick up speed.

This project is a long way from reality. But it shows how scientists are searching for new ways to explore interstellar space. Sending missions beyond the solar system could lead to exciting discoveries about the universe.

4

TRAVELING TO INTERSTELLAR SPACE

B y the 2020s, humans had traveled no farther than the Moon. There are currently no plans for human interstellar missions. The technology is not advanced enough. People would not be able to survive the long journey. Crewed missions beyond the solar system would need supplies for many years. They would need to carry food, water, and oxygen. Additionally, the conditions of space can harm health. Scientists are not sure how living in space for years might affect people.

Scientists hope that one day people will be able to journey beyond the solar system.

Apollo 17 was the last crewed mission to the Moon in the 1900s.

It may be a long time before these missions become possible. But this research could pave the way for future space travel.

LIFE SUPPORT SYSTEMS

Life support systems keep humans alive in space. The International Space Station (ISS) orbits the Earth. Machines on the ISS recycle oxygen and water. The life support system maintains air pressure and temperature in the station. It deals with waste and detects problems like fires.

Life support systems have limits. The ISS is good at recycling resources, but

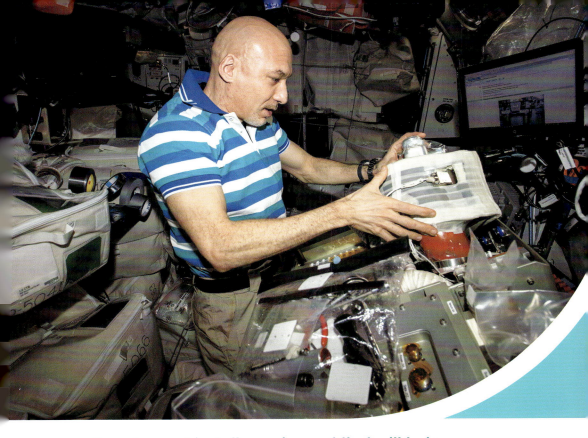

An astronaut installs equipment that will help remove carbon dioxide from the ISS.

astronauts on board still need things from Earth. Cargo spacecraft regularly send supplies to the space station. They deliver water, oxygen, food, and spare parts. Astronauts on the ISS have experimented with growing plants. But they are unable to grow enough food to survive.

Gisela Detrell studies life support systems. She is looking at microalgae. These small plants can remove carbon dioxide and create oxygen for astronauts. This could mean fewer cargo spacecraft from Earth are needed. This will be especially important for long missions. Interstellar ships might be too far away to receive shipments. Detrell says, "To further reduce the dependency on resupply from Earth, as many resources as possible should be recycled on board."[5]

Experiments on the ISS test the effects of space on microalgae.

SUSPENDED ANIMATION

One way to keep astronauts alive

for interstellar missions might be

suspended animation. Astronauts would

be put into a deep sleep. They would

need fewer resources to stay alive. This technology does not currently exist. But scientists are studying whether it might work.

Matteo Cerri is a scientist at the University of Bologna in Italy. He is exploring a form of suspended animation. He compares it to hibernation in animals. For example, some bears hibernate in the winter. Cerri says, "The core characteristic of hibernation is that you suddenly stop consuming energy."[6]

Space travelers in suspended animation would need less food, water, and oxygen.

Scientists study hibernating animals, such as bears, to learn whether hibernation is possible for humans.

Suspended animation might have other benefits too. Humans on long space trips have muscle and bone problems. Their muscles lose strength from lack of use. Their bones lose density. Animals in hibernation do not lose bone and muscle. Scientists are still learning more about why this is.

Scientists are also studying how emergency rooms use cold temperatures to keep people alive. Doctors sometimes cool down a person after a medical emergency. This reduces the risk of brain damage. It also causes the body's systems to slow down. This treatment lasts for only about twenty-four hours. Scientists do not know if long-term cooling is safe.

SPACE COLONIES

Some scientists want to build **colonies**

beyond the solar system. These would

be huge structures in space. One idea is

for a colony shaped like a huge cylinder.

It would be miles long. People would live

on the inside of the cylinder. The colony

BIOSPHERE 2

In 1991, eight researchers entered Biosphere 2. This sealed building was like a miniature Earth. It had a rain forest, desert, and wetlands. The researchers stayed inside Biosphere 2 for two years. They did research and farmed. The experiment helped scientists learn about creating a **sustainable** environment. A similar design could be used for a space colony in the future.

would spin around, creating a force like gravity. Space colonies like this will not be possible for a long time. The technologies needed to support a space colony are still being developed.

A space colony will need to be fully sustainable. Resources like oxygen and water will need to be totally recyclable. Colonists will need to be able to grow their own food. This will require advanced life support systems.

Future colonies may even be on other planets. The galaxy contains billions of stars. Many of them have their own planets.

Planets beyond the solar system may have conditions that are similar to Earth.

Some of those planets could be suitable for human life. Scientists have used telescopes to find many planets around other stars. It will take more work to learn if people could live on them. Traveling to these worlds would be very difficult. This would be the ultimate mission of space exploration beyond the solar system.

GLOSSARY

atmosphere

the layer of gas surrounding a planet or moon

colonies

regions or structures in a new or distant area intended for human life

data

information collected for study

interstellar space

the region of space that lies beyond the heliosphere

magnify

to make something appear larger

orbits

moves in a round path around another object in space

sustainable

able to be used for a long period of time without being used up

transmit

to send out a signal, especially through radio waves

SOURCE NOTES

CHAPTER ONE: EXPLORING WITH TELESCOPES

1. Quoted in Francis Reddy, "NASA's First Stellar Observatory, OAO 2, Turns 50," *NASA*, December 11, 2018. www.nasa.gov.

2. Quoted in "Interview with Sandra Irish, SWE Member & James Webb Space Telescope NASA Mechanical Systems Lead Structures Engineer," *SWE*, January 24, 2022. https://alltogether.swe.org.

CHAPTER TWO: EXPLORING WITH PROBES

3. Quoted in "Exploring the Solar System Through the Eyes of Robotic Voyagers," *NPR*, February 21, 2015. www.npr.org.

CHAPTER THREE: WHAT'S NEXT IN INTERSTELLAR EXPLORATION?

4. Quoted in Jonathan Amos, "Interstellar Probe: A Mission for the Generations," *BBC*, December 21, 2021. www.bbc.com.

CHAPTER FOUR: TRAVELING TO INTERSTELLAR SPACE

5. Quoted in Melissa Gaskill, "Building Better Life Support Systems for Future Space Travel," *NASA*, April 26, 2019. www.nasa.gov.

6. Quoted in Kate Baggaley, "'Cryosleep' May Open the Door to Deep Space. Here's How," *NBC News*, June 12, 2017. www.nbcnews.com.

FOR FURTHER RESEARCH

BOOKS

John Hamilton, *Hubble Space Telescope: Photographing the Universe.* Minneapolis, MN: Abdo, 2018.

Walt K. Moon, *Rockets and Space Travel.* San Diego, CA: BrightPoint Press, 2023.

Tamra B. Orr, *Space Discoveries.* North Mankato, MN: Capstone, 2019.

INTERNET SOURCES

Patchen Barss, "The Weird Space That Lies Outside Our Solar System," *BBC News*, September 8, 2020. www.bbc.com.

"Interstellar Mission," *NASA*, n.d. https://voyager.jpl.nasa.gov.

Vanessa Romo, "The James Webb Telescope Reaches Its Final Destination in Space, a Million Miles Away," *NPR*, January 24, 2022. www.npr.org.

WEBSITES

Deep Space Map
www.deepspacemap.com

Deep Space Map shows views of all visible galaxies, stars, and constellations. It is an interactive web app for astronomy. Most of the images come from the Hubble Space Telescope.

HubbleSite
https://hubblesite.org

HubbleSite is the official website of the Hubble Space Telescope. It shares news, images, and videos of what lies beyond the solar system.

National Aeronautics and Space Administration (NASA)
www.nasa.gov

NASA shares information about past, current, and future missions. It also shares image galleries and videos collected in space.

INDEX

IMAGE CREDITS

ABOUT THE AUTHOR

Christine Marie Layton is an author and educator. She writes nonfiction books and articles for children and young adults. Christine teaches language arts and English to culturally and linguistically diverse learners. She lives and works in Colorado Springs, Colorado.